W9-BVD-619

Everything You Need to Know

WHEN SOMEONE YOU LOVE HAS ALZHEIMER'S DISEASE

The intellectual and social abilities of the Alzheimer's patient steadily decline.

• THE NEED TO KNOW LIBRARY •

Everything You Need to Know

WHEN SOMEONE YOU LOVE HAS

ALZHEIMER'S DISEASE

Joyce Hinnefeld

THE ROSEN PUBLISHING GROUP, INC.
NEW YORK

Published in 1994 by The Rosen Publishing Group, Inc.
29 East 21st Street, New York, NY 10010

First Edition
Copyright 1994 by The Rosen Publishing Group, Inc.

Printed in Canada

Library of Congress Cataloging-in-Publication Data

Hinnefeld, Joyce.
    Everything you need to know when someone you love has
Alzheimer's disease / Joyce Hinnefeld.
        p.   cm. (The Need to know library)
    Includes bibliographical references and index.
    ISBN 0-8239-1688-X
    1. Alzheimer's disease—Juvenile literature. [1. Alzheimer's
disease.] I. Title. II. Series.
RC523.2.2H56 1994
616.8'31—dc20   93-44301
                                                CIP
                                                AC

Contents

Introduction

*P*edro, Sandra, and Jordan sit in a small lounge in the Sunset Harbor Nursing Home. Each of them is feeling a little nervous. They have come to this meeting at Sunset Harbor because they want to learn more about Alzheimer's disease. Ms. Jameson, a social worker at the home, has organized this teen support group meeting.

"Pedro," Ms. Jameson says after they have all introduced themselves, "why don't you get us started. Do you know someone with Alzheimer's disease?"

Pedro, who is only 13, clears his throat. He speaks in a quiet voice.

"Well, I think so. But I'm not really sure. Mrs. Nolan has lived across the hall from us since before I *was born. She took care of me sometimes when I was a baby. Lots of times after school I would stop by her apartment. She gave me cookies and we talked.*

"But lately something seems wrong. A couple weeks ago I ran into her on the street. She looked really confused, and at first she didn't recognize me. And last week I knocked on her door one day after school. She only opened the door a crack. She looked out and told me to go away."

"My grandmother does things like that, too," 14-year-old Sandra pipes up. Her eyes look sad as she begins to tell her story.

"At first my mom thought she was just depressed. But it got worse. She wasn't taking care of herself at all. So my mom persuaded her to move in with us.

"That was when we realized there was something really wrong. My Grandma Rosa never used to leave her house after dark. One time, after she came to live with us, my dad heard a noise outside in the middle of the night. Grandma Rosa was wandering around in our backyard. She told my dad she'd gone for a walk. But she said she couldn't find her way back to the house."

Mrs. Jameson turns to Jordan. "How about you, Jordan? Do these stories sound familiar?"

Jordan, who is 15 and very tall, fidgets a bit in his chair. "Yeah," he says. "My grandfather did some of those things early on. Now he's in this nursing home. He can't get out of bed anymore. When I go to see him, he doesn't even know who I am.

"I feel really bad for my little sister. At least I can remember my grandfather when he was healthy. We used to have fun together. We went fishing a lot. But my sister was a baby when we found out my grandfather had Alzheimer's disease. She's never known him any other way."

Alzheimer's disease can strike people as young as 40. But it is more common in people over the age of 65. People with Alzheimer's might live as long as 15 or 20 years after they are diagnosed. But the disease will cause many difficult changes in their lives. These changes will also be difficult for their families and friends.

This book will tell you more about Alzheimer's disease. It will tell you more about Pedro's neighbor Mrs. Nolan, Sandra's grandmother, and Jordan's grandfather. And it will tell you what you can do if someone you know has Alzheimer's.

Chapter 1

What Is Alzheimer's Disease?

It is estimated that in the United States nearly 2 million people over the age of 65 have Alzheimer's disease. This disease becomes more common as people get older. Some experts believe that as many as 20 percent of people over the age of 80 have Alzheimer's.

Doctors do not know what causes Alzheimer's disease, and there is no cure for it. In the United States, approximately 100,000 people die of illnesses related to Alzheimer's each year. It is the fourth or fifth leading cause of death. In this chapter we will look more closely at this disease that affects the lives of so many people.

History and Research

Alzheimer's disease is named after a German *neurologist* (a doctor who specializes in the brain and the nervous system) named Alois Alzheimer.

In 1907, Dr. Alzheimer described unusual symptoms in a 51-year-old woman who was his patient. She had a very poor memory, and she often got lost in the institution where she was a patient. Her symptoms grew worse over the next several years. She became depressed, and she began to have *hallucinations.* (Hallucinations are imaginary sights and sounds that seem real to the person who sees and hears them.)

After this woman's death, Dr. Alzheimer carefully examined her brain. He found that her brain had *atrophied* (wasted away, becoming much smaller in size). Under a microscope, he discovered various kinds of abnormalities in the cells.

Doctors today find similar signs in the brain of people who have died of Alzheimer's disease. They also sometimes find large amounts of aluminum in the tissues of the brain. This discovery has led some people to believe that aluminum is somehow responsible for the disease. But, to date, there has been no scientific proof of this.

Doctors and researchers do not know what causes Alzheimer's disease. Some researchers are looking for a possible *hereditary*, or *genetic*, pattern. These researchers look for clues, or *markers*, within the genes of people who have Alzheimer's.

Repeated forgetfulness, like misplacing house keys and not knowing which ones to use, may be the first sign of Alzheimer's disease.

Other researchers are looking for signs of a shortage of certain chemicals in the brain. One such chemical is called *acetylcholine*. Acetylcholine is needed for the transmission of messages in the brain and nervous system. Most researchers agree that Alzheimer's disease is probably caused by both genetic and chemical factors.

Dementia: The Diagnosis of Alzheimer's Disease

Alzheimer's disease causes many symptoms. Taken all together, these symptoms are referred to as *dementia*. The term *dementia* comes from the Latin word for madness or insanity. But people with the symptoms of dementia are not really mad.

Dementia refers to a serious loss of brain functions, such as thinking and remembering. The loss of these abilities creates problems with the tasks of everyday life. Many people grow more forgetful as they get older. But the thinking and memory loss caused by dementia are so serious that they make it difficult for a person to function at all.

Dementia itself is not a disease. It is a group of symptoms that may be caused by a number of different diseases or disorders. Researchers have estimated that dementia may be caused by more than 60 types of disorders. Examples of these disorders include *stroke* (an interruption in the flow of blood to the brain), pneumonia (fluid in the lungs), brain tumors, and lifelong alcoholism.

Many of these possible causes of dementia are treatable, and some can even be cured. But so far there is no cure for Alzheimer's disease. For this reason, doctors must be careful to test for many other possible illnesses before they diagnose Alzheimer's. If the symptoms are caused by another, treatable disorder, treatment for that disorder should begin right away. (Chapter 3 of this book provides more information on the diagnosis of people with Alzheimer's disease.)

Alzheimer's disease can strike adults in middle age, but it may be more difficult to recognize.

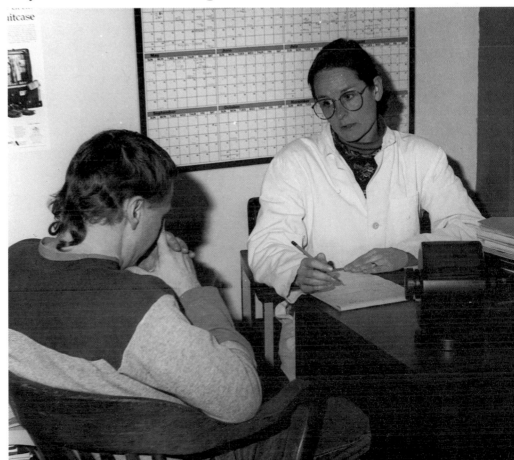

Symptoms

There is no cure for Alzheimer's disease. So people who care for Alzheimer's patients must find ways to deal with the symptoms of the dementia caused by the disease. You will learn about these symptoms in more detail later in this book. But here is a brief list of some of the symptoms commonly caused by Alzheimer's disease.

Severe memory problems. All of us forget things from time to time. But memory loss in the Alzheimer's patient can lead to serious problems at work or at home. A person with Alzheimer's may forget to do important tasks at his or her job or forget to turn off the stove or a faucet.

Poor judgment. Alzheimer's patients may make decisions that put themselves or others in danger. A person with Alzheimer's disease may think it is all right to drive a car, even though he or she can no longer drive safely.

Problems with abstract thinking. Alzheimer's patients may have trouble with symbols. Their reading and writing skills may decline. And they may lose the ability to use numbers, which can cause problems when it comes to dialing a phone, or changing a TV channel.

Signs of mental decline. Alzheimer's patients may show signs of a decline in their mental abilities. For example, they may have problems with language, recognition of objects or people, and motor skills. Doctors and researchers use terms

like *agnosia, anomia, aphasia,* and *apraxia* to refer
to these symptoms. These signs of mental decline
are discussed in more detail in Chapter 4 of this
book.

Personality and behavioral changes. People
with Alzheimer's disease may become hostile,
depressed, or extremely nervous. They sometimes
do things, like lying or stealing, that they would
never have done before.

Self-neglect. People with Alzheimer's disease
often stop taking care of themselves physically.
They may stop bathing, washing their clothes, and
eating properly.

Physical deterioration. Eventually, the
Alzheimer's patient begins to decline physically.
This may happen quickly, or it may progress slowly
over a number of years. Alzheimer's patients eventually die of physical ailments of some kind. The
most common causes of death are pneumonia,
urinary infections, and *decubiti* (sores caused by
being confined to a bed for a long period of time).

How Long Does It Last?

For some people, the symptoms of Alzheimer's
disease appear and get worse very quickly. This is
especially true for people who contract the disease
at a younger age (under 60, for example). These
people generally die within four to seven years.

When Alzheimer's disease begins at a later age,
the disease often develops more slowly. For these

people the symptoms appear and grow worse at a much slower rate. People of this age may live for as long as 20 years after being diagnosed with Alzheimer's disease.

At one time, researchers distinguished between these two forms of the disease. They referred to the more rapid form in younger people as *presenile dementia*. The slower form, more common in older patients, was referred to as *senile dementia*.

But researchers no longer use such terms. They also do not think of the two forms as separate diseases. Instead, they distinguish between Type I and Type II of Alzheimer's disease. Type I, which occurs in people over the age of 65, develops more slowly. Type II usually occurs between the ages of 45 and 55. Patients with Type II decline and die much more quickly.

Most researchers have thought that Type II Alzheimer's is more likely to be *inherited* (to occur within the same family). But recent research indicates that Type I of the disease may be related to a certain gene that is present in people who have the disease. This means that Type I of Alzheimer's disease may also be inherited.

Alzheimer's is very difficult, both for the patients who have it and for their families and friends. In the following chapters we will learn more about the difficulties these people face. We will begin with the story of Pedro and his neighbor, Mrs. Nolan.

Where Was I Going?

After Pedro, Sandra, and Jordan had introduced themselves, Ms. Jameson asked them to talk more about why they had come to this meeting about Alzheimer's disease. "Pedro," she said, "why don't you go first. If your neighbor Mrs. Nolan does have Alzheimer's disease, it sounds like she is in the early stage of the disease."

Pedro's Story

One day on my way to school, I saw Mrs. Nolan walking outside our building. I thought she was on her way to the candy store a few blocks away. She's worked there in the mornings for a long time. She was walking really slowly, and I ran to catch up with her to say hello.

It reminded me of when I was younger, and I would walk to the store with her in the morning on my way to school. Some mornings she'd open up and give me a piece of candy before I went on. But once I started junior high, I stopped walking with her. I always left later than she did in the morning because my new school was a lot closer.

So it seemed kind of funny that she was leaving so late and walking so slowly. When I caught up to her, I could see she had a worried look on her face.

"Hi, Mrs. Nolan," I said. "Is everything okay?"

She looked at me like I'd scared her. It seemed like she didn't recognize me at first. Then, when she finally figured out who I was, she grabbed my arm.

"Pedro," she said, "where was I going?"

I walked with her the rest of the way to the candy store and helped her open up. By the time she was all set up behind the cash register, she was laughing. She kept saying, "Pedro, I'm so sorry. That was so silly of me. I don't know what came over me."

But I didn't think it was funny. Because too many other things had been going wrong with Mrs. Nolan. There were other times when she hadn't recognized me at all and told me to go away.

I was late for school that morning. My teacher, Mr. Hauser, could tell I was upset, and he asked me what was wrong. When I told him about Mrs. Nolan, he said he'd see if he could find somebody I could talk to about it. The next day he told me about this meeting at Sunset Harbor.

Household chores and responsibilities are often neglected by the Alzheimer's patient.

An angry word from a loved one with Alzheimer's can confuse and upset a young child.

Alzheimer's Disease: Stage 1

Doctors and researchers often describe three stages that most patients with Alzheimer's disease go through. As Ms. Jameson pointed out to Pedro, Sandra, and Jordan, not everyone with Alzheimer's goes through each of these stages. And not everyone with the disease will have all the symptoms associated with each stage.

But knowing about these three stages can help you understand how the disease develops. It can also give you some idea of what to expect if someone you know is diagnosed with Alzheimer's.

Stage 1 of Alzheimer's disease generally lasts for around one to three years. In many cases, people with the disease are not even diagnosed until they are well into the first stage.

The most obvious symptom of Stage 1 is the loss of memory. As was mentioned before, many people have trouble remembering things, and this often gets worse as people get older. But people in the first stage of the disease have trouble remembering even recent events. For example, a person with Alzheimer's might forget what his or her boss asked for just a few minutes before. That kind of memory loss can lead to serious problems at work.

Related to this memory loss is a confusion about places. An Alzheimer's patient may get lost on the way to work, for example. Think of Mrs. Nolan, who had to ask Pedro where she was going. People with Alzheimer's get lost even in familiar places because the disease makes it difficult for them to recognize or remember familiar things.

Alzheimer's sufferers may also have trouble handling money. This may be related to memory loss. Patients may simply forget which bills they have paid and which they haven't paid.

In the first stage of Alzheimer's a patient may seem tired or depressed. In fact, sometimes Alzheimer's is confused with depression, at least at first. And patients may also undergo changes in mood or personality. Patients become withdrawn and silent. They may occasionally have angry outbursts, even if that is something they never would have done before. Pedro was surprised, for instance, when Mrs. Nolan told him to go away when he knocked on her door. In the past she had always been happy to see him.

Another problem that often happens in the early stage of the disease is difficulty in making judgments and calculations. For example, a person may have trouble judging time and distance. This kind of trouble can cause serious problems, and hazards, with driving. Family members and friends of Alzheimer's patients often become concerned about the driving abilities of their loved ones. Often, patients must be prevented from driving at all. This can be a painful process for family members or friends.

At Stage 1, Alzheimer's patients generally know that something is wrong. But they may have trouble coping with that knowledge. It may make them even more upset and nervous to realize that they are unable to control certain parts of their lives. This realization is painful and upsetting for their friends and family members as well.

In the next chapter we will talk more about how Alzheimer's is diagnosed. We will also discuss some of the things that can be done to help Alzheimer's patients feel safe and secure and be as happy as possible.

Chapter **3**

Diagnosing and Caring for Alzheimer's Patients

The process of diagnosing Alzheimer's disease is usually begun by the family members of patients, rather than the patients themselves. Often there is one critical event or experience that prompts family members to begin the process. As we have seen, an Alzheimer's patient may start getting lost on the way to work. Someone who has always handled money very carefully may suddenly lose the ability to balance a checkbook. Another person who has always taken pride in his or her appearance may stop bathing and start dressing sloppily.

Diagnosing the Problem

Doctors will usually want to know as much as possible about the patient's history. They will be especially interested in memory loss. They will want to know whether the patient's memory has declined gradually over a period of time, or whether it has been abrupt and sudden. The onset of Alzheimer's is slow and gradual. If a person has lost his or her memory abruptly, the problem is more likely to be a stroke.

Remember that dementia, the loss of intellectual abilities associated with Alzheimer's disease, can be caused by over 60 different disorders. If a patient shows symptoms of dementia, the process of diagnosis should begin as soon as possible. It is important to look for other possible causes of the dementia. Unlike Alzheimer's, these other causes might be treatable.

Friends and family members should also remember that no single sign or symptom shows up in every case. There is no automatic, foolproof evidence that a person has Alzheimer's.

But doctors can usually make a fairly accurate diagnosis based on three factors. These are: (1) the patient's history, (2) the medical history of the patient's family, and (3) a full medical examination. There are other tests that doctors perform to make their diagnosis even more accurate. These tests include the following:

• A *CAT (computerized axial tomography) scan.* In a CAT scan, a large number of X-ray photographs are taken of the patient's brain. These X rays are then put together by a computer, in order to provide a more complete picture of the brain.

It is important for Alzheimer's patients to get regular, supervised exercise.

An Alzheimer's patient may prefer finger foods at mealtimes.

• An *EEG (electroencephalogram)*. An EEG provides a record of the electrical activity, or waves, in the patient's brain.
   • Various tests of the patient's mental abilities.
   • Various blood tests.

Treatment

There is no cure for Alzheimer's disease, and there is really no way to treat the disease itself. Sometimes, however, doctors prescribe medication to help patients and caregivers deal with some of the symptoms of the disease, which can include:
   • anxiety
   • depression
   • hallucinations and delusions
   • aggressive behavior
No medication (prescription or over-the-counter) should be given to Alzheimer's patients without consulting their doctor.

One symptom that can pose serious dangers for Alzheimer's patients is their tendency to wander, especially at night. Experts on the disease recommend certain techniques for dealing with this. For example, they suggest allowing the patient to walk in a safe, fenced-in space. They also recommend that caregivers take long walks with Alzheimer's patients. Sometimes it may be necessary to install alarms or tricky locks to prevent patients from wandering outside on their own.

Caring for the Patient

Although there is no cure and no complete treatment for Alzheimer's, there are things that can be done to ease the burden of the disease. Caregivers should remember that Alzheimer's patients are confused and frightened. They are losing control over their lives, and this makes them anxious and fearful.

Caregivers should also keep in mind the self-esteem of Alzheimer's patients. It is very difficult to lose control over one's life in this way. And it may be embarrassing and shameful to Alzheimer's patients to lose the ability to care for themselves.

There are a number of things that can be done to ease the fear and anxiety of Alzheimer's patients. First, efforts can be made to communicate with the patient, even when he or she is losing regular language skills. Medical experts often refer to this as "speaking the patient's language." Second, a number of things can be done to create a safe and pleasant living environment for someone who has Alzheimer's.

Many books and articles are available on caring for people with Alzheimer's. If someone in your family has the disease, chances are other family members may be involved in caring for that person. Perhaps you will help with this caregiving, too. As we will learn in Chapter 5, one of the most difficult things about Alzheimer's is deciding how to care for the patient.

Alzheimer's patients need love and reassurance from their caregivers.
They respond well to a warm smile and a pleasant manner.

But even if you are not directly involved in caring for someone with the disease, you might be interested in some of the things that must be done. The two boxes that follow list some important steps for friends, family members, and caregivers to keep in mind when caring for patients.

Creating a Safe and Pleasant Living Environment

1. Make sure the patient gets exercise, such as a daily walk, for as long as possible.
2. Avoid crowds, and reduce noise (from television, radios, telephones, and so forth) as much as possible.
3. Use locks and alarms on doors if needed. Keep dangerous objects or materials in cabinets with safety latches.
4. Try to reduce clutter, and keep hallways as clear as possible. Try not to have too many mirrors on the walls, because sometimes it frightens Alzheimer's patients to see themselves in mirrors. Provide familiar objects, such as a favorite pillow or old photographs, for the patient.
5. Make dressing simple for the patient. One way to do this is to get rid of clothing with complicated ties, buttons, and so forth. Establish a regular routine for washing, brushing teeth, and going to the bathroom.
6. Prepare simple foods, and give the patient one item at a time. If the patient has trouble using eating utensils, prepare sandwiches and finger foods.
7. Provide the patient with things to do under supervision, such as arts and crafts activities, or simple cooking or cleaning tasks.

Communication: Speaking the Patient's Language

1. Touch the patient often, and use eye contact. This will help the patient feel loved and secure.
2. Do not rely on words alone. Use gestures when you are trying to communicate with the patient.
3. Pay attention to the patient's body language.
4. When the patient is calm and at rest, take advantage of those moments to express your love and concern.
5. Listen to the patient when he or she speaks, even if the words do not make sense.
6. When you speak to the patient, keep your voice calm and low. Give the patient lots of time to listen and respond to what you say.

Pedro and Mrs. Nolan

After hearing about the process of diagnosing Alzheimer's disease, Pedro made some decisions. First, he planned to ask Mrs. Nolan when she had had her last doctor's appointment. He would encourage her to go in for a checkup, and he would offer to ride with her on the bus to her doctor's office. He would try to remember that she was probably frightened by the things that were happening to her and maybe embarrassed. "I'll talk as calmly as I can. I'll try to be really reassuring," he said.

But even more important, Pedro was going to encourage his mother to call Mrs. Nolan's son. "If I were her son," Pedro said, "I would want to know. I would want to do whatever I could to help my mother."

Alzheimer's patients may wander at night.

Chapter 4

Grandma Rosa's Nighttime Walks

When Pedro finished his story about Mrs. Nolan, Sandra spoke up. "I think it's great that you're trying to find out now what's wrong with Mrs. Nolan. For a long time we thought there wasn't really anything wrong with my Grandma Rosa. By the time we realized she had Alzheimer's disease, her symptoms were a lot worse. I think she's in the second stage of the disease now."

Sandra's Story

My Grandpa Carl died four years ago, when I was ten. For a long time after he died, Grandma Rosa cried every day. It seemed like she would never get over losing him. She had no energy at all, and she never wanted to do anything or go anywhere.

Eventually Grandma Rosa started forgetting things. She only lived ten blocks from our house. But one evening she got lost driving home after she'd been at our house for dinner. And she stopped paying her bills, too. My mom had to start taking care of all her banking and other money matters.

Like I said, this went on for a long time. But we just thought she was depressed because of losing Grandpa Carl. We thought that was what was making her careless and forgetful and tired all the time.

One day, one of Grandma Rosa's neighbors, Mrs. Thompson, called. She said she was worried about Grandma. She said she had seen Grandma Rosa getting into her car in her pajamas. When she went outside to ask her where she was going, Grandma Rosa said she couldn't remember. Mrs. Thompson took her back into her house and called my mom.

My mom decided that it was time for Grandma Rosa to move in with us. It wasn't easy to get her to move, either. She and Grandpa Carl had lived in the same house for forty years, and she didn't want to leave it. She got really mad at my mom and yelled at her. That upset my mom a lot. Finally, though, she agreed to move in.

Once she was living with us, we started to notice a lot of things that seemed wrong. For one thing, she didn't like to take baths or showers, and her clothes were always sloppy and stained. That didn't make any sense, because Grandma Rosa had always been neat as a pin.

And then there was the night my dad found her wandering around outside the house. That was when we knew something serious was happening. Grandma Rosa had always been afraid to leave the house after dark. But there she was wandering around outside, telling my dad she was going for a walk.

So my mom took her to the hospital for all kinds of tests. They tested for everything, and finally they decided that she had Alzheimer's disease.

It's so hard on my mom. She feels like it was her fault that we didn't realize it was Alzheimer's disease for so long. And taking care of Grandma Rosa is really wearing her out. She can't even talk to my grandma about it, because Grandma Rosa thinks there's nothing wrong with her.

Alzheimer's Disease: Stage 2

The second stage of Alzheimer's disease can last anywhere from 2 to 10 years after the disease is diagnosed. Memory loss becomes much worse during this stage. Patients have trouble remembering both recent events and events from earlier in their lives.

During this stage of the disease there are signs of significant mental decline. When they reach the second stage, people with Alzheimer's usually display two or more of the following symptoms:

Agnosia. Patients with agnosia are unable to recognize familiar objects or people. A person with Alzheimer's may not be able to distinguish between

The Alzheimer's patient will eventually have trouble doing even simple, everyday tasks.

a pencil and a fork. Similarly, patients are often unable to recognize family members and people they've known for many years.

Anomia. Anomia refers to difficulty in remembering the word or name for an object. A patient may have trouble thinking of the word *fork*, for example. Instead, he or she might refer to a fork as "the thing you eat with."

Aphasia. Aphasia refers to problems with using language. Alzheimer's patients often have trouble speaking and understanding language. They often arrange words in the wrong order.

Apraxia. Patients with apraxia have trouble with perceptual and motor coordination. They may have trouble with things like setting the table. Even getting in and out of chairs, washing, or feeding themselves may be difficult. This is not because of muscle weakness or a lack of coordination. Rather, it is the result of a decline in the brain's ability to coordinate such activities.

In Stage 2, patients are often restless. They want to wander or walk about, especially in the late afternoon or at night. Think of Sandra's Grandma Rosa and her nighttime walks. Occasionally, patients at this stage may experience *seizures* (sudden attacks that sometimes cause a person's body to twitch or jerk). They may also experience a change in the way they walk. For example, they may begin to limp or drag one foot because of increased muscular tension.

These patients often have difficulty reading, writing, and working with numbers. They may have trouble dealing with money, not just because of memory problems, but because they are unable to do simple addition and subtraction.

Patients in the second stage of Alzheimer's often become sloppy. They may no longer care about bathing or taking care of themselves and their clothing. Bathing may also be threatening or diffi-cult for them because of apraxia. Some patients have huge appetites and gain a great deal of weight. Eventually, they will probably lose interest in food and will lose weight rapidly.

At this stage of the disease, patients' moods become even more unpredictable. They may be suspicious and irritable one day, restless and silly or sad and tearful the next. They usually have no awareness of their condition.

This lack of awareness can be very hard on friends, family members, and caregivers. They must deal with the patient's illness on their own, knowing that the patient does not know what is happening to him or her. By the second stage of the disease, the Alzheimer's patient may seem to be a completely different person.

In the next chapter we will talk about things family members and caregivers can do for Alzheimer's patients. We will also discuss the difficulty and stress that go along with caring for someone with this disease.

Chapter 5

The Strain of Dealing with Alzheimer's Disease

The friends and family members of someone with Alzheimer's should learn as much about the disease as they can. And they should learn about it as soon as they can. There are many preparations to be made when someone you know is suffering the symptoms.

Often, one person becomes the main caregiver for an Alzheimer's patient, at least at first. This may be the husband or wife of the patient, or perhaps a son or daughter.

Caregiver Support

Being the main caregiver for someone with Alzheimer's can be very stressful. Counselors and therapists who work with caregivers report that caregivers often experience symptoms of their own. These symptoms include:

- depression
- anger and frustration
- worry and anxiety

Alzheimer's caregivers need a great deal of support. This support usually comes from two sources: (1) the family, and (2) the community, or social services.

Family Support. If someone in your family has Alzheimer's, it may be difficult for everyone. Some family members may feel guilty because they are too far away to help. Other family members who live closer to the patient may feel that it is unfair for them to have to take on so much responsibility. If one of your parents or grandparents is the main caregiver for someone with Alzheimer's, you may sometimes feel jealous because you've been deprived of the caregiver's time and attention.

It is often difficult to admit that we have feelings like these. When someone is ill, we want to be caring and supportive. But usually it is best for family members also to be honest with one another about what they are feeling and what they need. Then they will be better able to help the patient and one another.

One way of being honest is for family members to go together to talk to a counselor or therapist about their feelings. It is especially important for the main caregiver to talk to a counselor.

Caring for a loved one with Alzheimer's requires support from the entire family.

Social Support. Friends and family members should start looking for support services in their community as soon as they learn that someone they love has Alzheimer's. This is especially true for the patient's main caregiver. Caregivers should always remember that they will take better care of the patient if they take care of *themselves,* too.

For help in locating social support within your community, you might contact one of the following:

• Gerontologists (doctors who specialize in the care of older people).

• Community mental health centers.

• Medical information and referral programs.

• Area agencies on aging. (Contact the Administration on Aging for the agency nearest you. The address and telephone number are listed under "Where to Get Help" on page 61 of this book.)

• Alzheimer's Resource and Information Centers. (The addresses and telephone numbers for several of these centers are also listed under "Where to Get Help.")

One important service that friends and family members should look for is a support group for families of Alzheimer's patients. In groups of this kind, caregivers and family members are able to come together to talk about the disease. Support groups provide a place for people to express their feelings. But they can also be an important place for learning about ways to deal with Alzheimer's more effectively on a day-to-day basis.

Ways of Caring

Among things friends and family members might learn about at support group meetings are different ways of providing care for Alzheimer's patients. Here are brief descriptions of a few types of care that might be available in your community.

Home health care. There are some services available to provide care for the Alzheimer's patient in his or her own home. Examples include "Meals on Wheels" (a service that brings food to the patient's home), homemaker services that provide cleaning and shopping, and home health aides who can help with the patient's medication and basic health care.

Adult day care. In some communities, there are adult day-care programs for people with Alzheimer's. These programs provide a place for patients to mix socially. But more important, they can provide caregivers with a rest from the strain of dealing with the disease and an opportunity to go to work. Adult day-care programs are still not available everywhere, and they may be rather expensive. But this is a rapidly growing form of care for Alzheimer's patients in the United States.

Respite care. Respite-care programs are temporary residential programs. They allow caregivers to place the patient in someone else's care, either in a special home or in another outside facility, for a brief time. Some families of people with Alzheimer's have joined together to form

Shopping or running errands for an Alzheimer's patient is a loving way to show that you care.

shared respite programs. In these programs, different families take turns caring for a small group of Alzheimer's patients for a brief time. For some patients and their families, respite-care programs can provide a way to begin preparing for full-time nursing home care.

Nursing home care. The decision to place a loved one in a nursing home is a difficult, often emotional one for many families. There is no correct answer about when this decision should be made. Every family must make its own decision, based on its own situation.

In most cases, Alzheimer's patients will eventually need full-time care, often in a nursing home. As you will learn in Chapter 6, patients in the last stage of Alzheimer's are usually not able to do anything for themselves. Families of Alzheimer's patients should begin making plans for the final stage of the disease as early as possible. That way, they will be able to make a careful decision about the best place for their loved one to be.

Some nursing homes now have special Alzheimer's disease units. These units provide activities for patients, who usually have a great deal of energy. They also provide security measures to keep patients from wandering away.

Besides activities and security, there are a number of other things for family members to look for when selecting a nursing home. Here are a few questions to ask:

• Are the doctors and nurses on the staff familiar with Alzheimer's disease? How do they interact with patients in the nursing home?

• Does the nursing home provide opportunities for the family to be involved in the patient's life? Are there support group meetings for family members?

• Are there safe places for patients to walk? Are they taken outside for a change of scenery?

• Is the atmosphere warm and friendly?

Sandra and Grandma Rosa

When Sandra left the meeting at Sunset Harbor Nursing Home, she had made several decisions. One was that she would do all she could to help and support her mother, who was Grandma Rosa's main caregiver. The second was that she would come back to the next teen support group meeting at Sunset Harbor Nursing Home. And the last was that she would encourage her mother to join one of the support groups for caregivers that also met at the nursing home.

Chapter 6

Granddad Doesn't Even See Me

"**I** know what you mean about not wanting your grandmother to go to a nursing home," Jordan said when Sandra finished her story about Grandma Rosa. "It was hard for my dad to make that decision. But they take good care of Granddad here at Sunset Harbor. And we don't live too far away, so we can visit him pretty often. What's hard now is that most of the time I don't think he even knows we're here. He's in the last stage of the disease, and he doesn't seem anything like the Granddad I used to know."

Jordan's Story

I don't really remember my grandmother. She died when I was a baby. But I have great memories of Granddad. He lived out in the country, and when

47

I was a little kid, I spent several weeks with him in the summer. We went fishing every day. He taught me everything I know about fishing. And he told the funniest jokes I've ever heard.

Granddad was diagnosed with Alzheimer's disease when I was eight. That was the year my baby sister Natasha was born. She never knew Granddad when he was normal.

Not too long after we found out about the disease, Granddad started doing some of the things Sandra talked about. He'd wander off at night, and he got lost a lot. He also started having seizures. His whole body would shake, and then get really stiff. I saw him having one once. It really upset me.

I didn't know what was happening, and I was scared. Finally one day I said to my dad, "Is Granddad about to die?"

He sat down with me and explained some things about Alzheimer's. And ever since then he's always let me know what's going on with Granddad.

Granddad's been sick for a long time. In the last few years he's gotten a whole lot worse. He can't get out of bed anymore. He really can't do anything for himself. He needs a nurse's help to go to the bathroom. Sometimes he can't even control that, and he makes a mess in the bed.

He's thin as a rail, even though they feed him three meals a day. He can't really say much, and he never seems to recognize anybody. I still come to visit him but it makes me really sad.

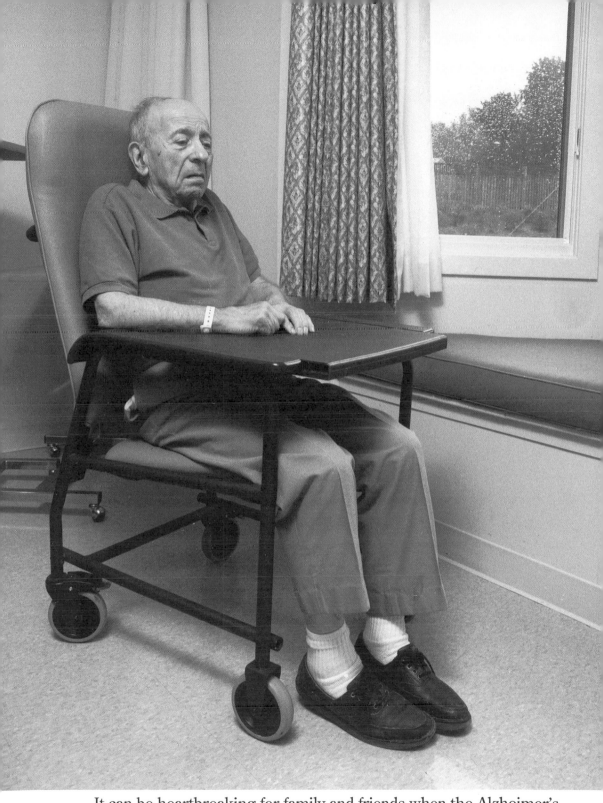

It can be heartbreaking for family and friends when the Alzheimer's patient they love no longer recognizes them.

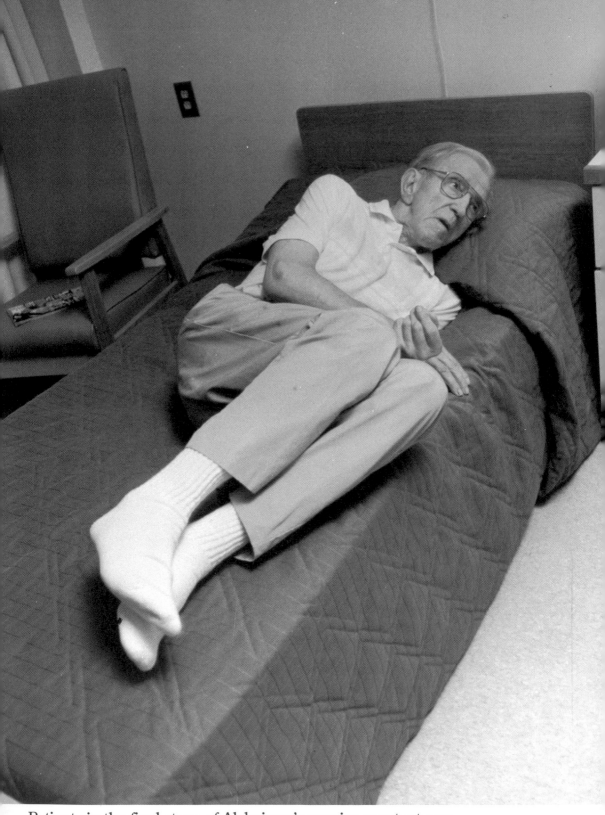

Patients in the final stage of Alzheimer's require constant care.

*He still has seizures sometimes. My dad says there
are days when he groans and screams almost all day.
When that happens my dad tells me to wait out in the
lounge.*

*The doctor says Granddad will be this way until
he dies. He says all we can do now is try to make
him as comfortable as we can. I was thinking the
other day that it almost seems like Granddad is turn-
ing back into a baby. He just lies in bed and sleeps
most of the time.*

*I came today because I want to figure out how to
explain all of this to my sister. I want her to know
what's happening to Granddad. And I want her to
know he wasn't always like this.*

Alzheimer's Disease: Stage 3

Stage 3 is the final stage of Alzheimer's disease.
It is hard to predict the length of this stage. As we
learned in Chapter 1, some people live for many
years after being diagnosed. For these people, this
stage could last for a long time, maybe as long as 8
to 12 years. But other people, especially those with
Type II Alzheimer's, grow much worse much more
quickly. For these people, this stage can be as
short as one to three years.

Patients in the third and final stage become
completely unable to care for themselves. The
symptoms of mental damage that appeared during
Stage 2 of the disease become even worse. (These
symptoms are described in Chapter 4.)

In the earlier stages, patients may occasionally have trouble recognizing people. But as they grow worse, in Stage 3, they may eventually not be able to recognize anyone at all. They may not even recognize themselves in a mirror. Think of Jordan, and his feeling that his grandfather could no longer even see him.

During Stage 3, Alzheimer's patients decline physically. They appear extremely weak and tired. They sleep a great deal. They spend most of their time in a chair or in bed. Eventually, the patient will simply lie curled up in bed.

Like Jordan's grandfather, patients in the final stage generally lose a great deal of weight, even when they are eating well. Some people may have seizures. Some make groaning, screaming, or grunting noises. Occasionally, a patient in the final stage will lapse into a coma (state of being unconscious) before death.

Patients in the final stage need constant care and supervision. Although these patients may live for a number of years, their friends and family know that they will eventually die. They must prepare themselves for the death of their loved ones, and for the grief that they will face. In the final chapter of this book, we will consider some stages of grief that friends and family members may go through.

Chapter 7

Losing Someone You Love

When someone you love has Alzheimer's, you must cope with the fact that that person will die. Family members and friends must adjust to this disease in the same way they would adjust to any terminal disease.

The psychologist Elisabeth Kübler-Ross has identified and described various stages of grief that family members go through when a loved one dies. In an article called "Helping Families Cope with Alzheimer's Disease," Paul Teusink and Susan Mahler apply Dr. Kübler-Ross's stages of grief to families who are dealing with Alzheimer's patients. In this chapter we will talk about these stages of adjustment.

Stages of Family Adjustment

Denial. Often, Alzheimer's patients do not want to admit that there is anything wrong with them. But sometimes family members and friends are reluctant to admit it, too. Because it is so painful to think of their loved one having the disease, they may deny it. In other words, they may pretend at first that it isn't true.

We now know that the symptoms of Alzheimer's get worse as patients go through the stages of the disease. Eventually friends and family members will no longer be able to deny that their loved one is seriously ill.

Overinvolvement. The next stage many friends and family members go through is overinvolvement. People in this stage, especially the main caregiver, try to make up for the disease by getting overinvolved in the patient's life. Some try to do everything for the patient, no matter what it takes.

But caregivers and other family members should not get so involved in patients' lives that their own lives suffer. Caregivers have needs, too. They must first take care of *themselves* in order to be able to care for Alzheimer's patients.

Anger. Sometimes friends and family members get angry when they realize that all their time and attention have not made the Alzheimer's patients any better. They may even get angry at the patients themselves.

It's never easy to deal with the death of a loved one.

Alzheimer's patients communicate differently. They are often frightened, confused, forgetful, and demanding. Caregivers may not know what to expect from one day to the next, and it is sometimes hard to always be understanding.

Also it is difficult for friends and family members to accept these changes in their loved one. But it is better for everyone if friends and family members can avoid showing anger or frustration to the patient.

Guilt. In the next stage of adjustment friends and family members often feel guilty. They may feel bad about getting angry, for example. But they need to remember that anger is a stage that most people go through in dealing with the disease.

Sometimes friends and family members feel guilty because they think they could have prevented the disease somehow. Or they may look back over the patient's life and wish they had treated him or her better at different times.

All of these reactions are normal. It is important for friends and family members to realize that they could not have prevented the disease in any way. Instead of thinking about past mistakes, they must look for ways to show their love and concern for the patient now.

Acceptance. Finding ways to show love and concern is a step toward the final stage of acceptance. When friends and family members reach this stage, they are finally at peace with the disease.

Collecting pictures of a loved one can help to keep his or her memory alive.

They understand that they could not have prevented their loved one from getting sick. And they know there is nothing they can do to make the disease go away. Instead, they will do their best to deal with the problems from day to day.

When someone you care about has Alzheimer's, you may feel things like anger and guilt, too. Try to remember that the best thing you can do is to find ways to comfort and help the patient. Look for ways to learn more about the disease. And do your best to be supportive of other friends and family members who are adjusting to the stress and the eventual loss of a loved one.

Jordan and His Grandfather

After the teen support group meeting at Sunset Harbor Nursing Home, Jordan decided he would definitely come back for the next meeting. He realized that it really helped him to talk to other people his own age who were trying to deal with the same problems and worries.

And Sandra and Pedro had also given him a very good idea. When he said he felt bad that his sister Natasha would never know what their grandfather was like before he got Alzheimer's, Sandra suggested he write down all his memories and experiences. Create his own book.

At first he laughed. "You're kidding!" he said. "Me write a book?"

"I'm serious," Sandra said. "You could write down all the things you remember about your grandfather. You could write about going to the farm, about fishing, all of that."

"That's a great idea," Pedro said. "And you could have a whole chapter on jokes! You could write down all the jokes your grandfather ever told you. And then they'd always be there for Natasha, and for you, too."

The more he thought about it, the more Jordan liked that idea. Writing down his memories of his grandfather would be a way of finally accepting the disease. It would also be the nicest way of keeping the memory of his grandfather alive for everyone in the family, year after year.

Glossary—*Explaining New Words*

acetylcholine A chemical needed for the transmission of messages in the brain.

agnosia Inability to recognize familiar objects or people.

anomia Difficulty in remembering the word or name for an object.

aphasia Problems with speaking and understanding language.

apraxia Problems with perceptual and motor coordination.

CAT (computerized axial tomography) scan A test in which a large number of X rays are taken of a person's brain and then put together by a computer.

dementia A group of symptoms that indicate a serious loss of *intellectual functions*, such as thinking and remembering.

EEG (electroencephalogram) A test that provides a record of the electrical activity, or waves, in a person's brain.

genetic A trait that has to do with a person's genes, and that is often passed from one generation of a family to the next.

gerontologist A doctor who specializes in the care of older people.

hallucinations Imaginary sights and sounds that seem real to the person who sees and hears them.

hereditary Something that is passed along from one generation of a family to the next; this term is related to the term *genetic.*

neurologist A doctor who specializes in the brain and nervous system.

respite care A form of care in which the patient stays in a temporary residential program; relief or rest for the main caregiver.

seizure Sudden attack that sometimes causes a person's body to twitch or jerk.

terminal disease An illness that will cause death.

Type I Alzheimer's disease A form of Alzheimer's disease that occurs in people over the age of 65 and develops slowly.

Type II Alzheimer's disease A form of Alzheimer's disease that usually occurs between the ages of 45 and 55 and develops more quickly than Type I Alzheimer's disease.

Where to Get Help

Contact these groups to get more information about Alzheimer's disease, and to learn about the different forms of care and support groups that are available in your community.

Administration on Aging
330 Independence Avenue
Washington, DC 20201
(202) 472-7257

Alzheimer's Disease and Related Disorders Association (Alzheimer's Association)
919 North Michigan Avenue
Suite 1000
Chicago, IL 60611-1676
(312) 335-8700   TDD (312) 335-8882
Information and Referral Service Line: 1-800-272-3900

Familial Alzheimer's Disease Research Foundation (Alzheimer's Foundation)
8177 South Harvard
Tulsa, OK 74137
(918) 631-3665

John Douglas French Foundation for Alzheimer's Disease
11620 Wilshire Boulevard
Los Angeles, CA 90025
(213) 470-5462

The National Resource Center on Alzheimer's Disease
USF Suncoast Gerontology Center
12901 Bruce B. Downs Boulevard
MDC Box 50
Tampa, FL 33617
(813) 974-4355

For Further Reading

Beckelman, Laurie. *Alzheimer's Disease.* New York: Crestwood House, 1990.

Check, William A. *Alzheimer's Disease.* New York: Chelsea House, 1989.

Frank, Julia. *Alzheimer's Disease: The Silent Epidemic.* Minneapolis: Lerner Publications Co., 1985.

Landau, Elaine. *Alzheimer's Disease.* New York: Franklin Watts, Inc., 1987.

Wilkinson, Beth. *Coping When a Grandparent Has Alzheimer's Disease.* New York: Rosen Publishing Group, 1992.

The Alzheimer's Association has numerous publications, including:
Alzheimer's Disease: Especially for Teenagers
Communicating with the Alzheimer Patient
If You Think Someone You Know Has Alzheimer's Disease
Grandpa Doesn't Know It's Me (an illustrated children's book)

An entire issue of *Aging* magazine, Numbers 363–364, 1992 is devoted to the subject of Alzheimer's disease. Published by the Administration on Aging in the United States Department of Health and Human Services.

Index

About the Author
Joyce Hinnefeld has worked as an editor for *World Book Encyclopedia* and in the college division of St. Martin's Press. She is also a fiction writer, and has taught writing at all levels. She lives in New York State.

Photo Credits
Cover photo by Stuart Rabinowitz.
Photo on page 13: Stuart Rabinowitz; all other photos by Norma Mondazzi.

Design/Production: Blackbirch Graphics, Inc.